BUYING A PROPERTY

Buy the right property, in the right place, for the right price

or

What you really need to know so that you don't make a costly and heart-breaking mistake

Jane Myers and Stuart Myers

Equiculture Publishing

Copyright © October 2014

ISBN: 978-0-9941561-2-9

Email: stuart@equiculture.com.au

Disclaimer

The authors and publisher shall have neither liability nor responsibility to any person or entity with respect to any loss or damage caused or alleged to be caused directly or indirectly by the information contained in this book. While the book is as accurate as the authors can make it, there may be errors, omissions and inaccuracies.

The purpose of this publication is to inform, not to advise. Your decisions or legal actions should be based on advice from a legal advisor or expert familiar with the specific facts relating to your property.

About this book

Buying a horse property is probably the most expensive and important purchase you will ever make. Therefore, it is very important that you get it right. There are many factors to consider and there may be compromises that have to be made. This guide to buying a horse property will help you to make many of those very important decisions.

Decisions include factors such as whether to buy developed or undeveloped land? Whether to buy a smaller property nearer the city or a larger property in a rural area? Other factors that you need to think about include the size and layout of the property, the pastures and soil, access to riding areas, the water supply, and any possible future proposals for the area. These subjects and many more are covered in this book.

A useful checklist is also provided so that you can ask the right questions before making this very important decision.

If you are buying a horse property, you cannot afford to miss out on the invaluable information in this book!

Thank you for buying this book and please consider either leaving a review or contacting us with feedback,
stuart@equiculture.com.au

About the authors

Jane Myers MSc (Equine Science) is the author of several professional books about horses including the best selling book **Managing Horses on Small Properties** (published by CSIRO).

Jane has lived and breathed horses from a young age and considers herself to be very fortunate in that she has been able to spend her life riding, training and studying these amazing animals.

Stuart Myers (BSc) has a background in human behaviour and has been a horse husband for more years than he cares to remember.

Jane and Stuart are particularly interested in sustainable horse-keeping practices and issues, such as low stress horse management that also delivers environmental benefits. They present workshops to horse owners in Australia, the USA and the UK about sustainable horse and horse property management as part of their business, **Equiculture**.

Their experience is second to none when it comes to this subject as they keep up with recent advances/research and are involved in research themselves. They travel the world as part of their work and they bring this information to you via their books, online resources and websites.

See the Equiculture website www.equiculture.com.au where you will find lots of great information about horsekeeping and please join the mailing list while you are there!

Jane and Stuart also have another website that supports their Horse Rider's Mechanic series of workbooks. This website is www.horseridersmechanic.com why not have a look?

Photo credits

All photos and diagrams by Jane Myers and Stuart Myers unless otherwise accredited. Any errors and omissions please let us know.

Contents

Very important lifestyle decisions

If you are in the very fortunate position of being able to buy your own horse property you have a lot of decisions to make so that you buy the right property, in the right place, for the right price.

Finally, after endless discussions with your other half and the rest of the family, you have persuaded them that what is needed to make everyone's life complete is a house on acreage out in the country where you can all live in perfect harmony with nature. You imagine yourself on a beautiful horse property, looking out of the window at your horses grazing peacefully on the lovely pasture, your partner, at one with the land on the tractor, your children playing safely in the garden away from busy roads. Just beyond the children, the family dog is playfully rounding up the chickens...

Equine utopia is what most horse owners dream about.

The flip side of this vision is that you look out of the window at your horses on bare, overgrazed pasture, trying to decide if you have the time, energy or motivation to transport one of them somewhere safe to ride (because you nearly had an accident the last time you rode out of your front gate). Your partner is trying in vain to repair the tractor after another long, hard week at work and you are wondering if they will also have the enthusiasm to repair some fences. Your children, who are bored of playing with one another, miss their school mates and are waiting for the family taxi (you) to take them to visit their friends, a long drive away; meanwhile the dog has killed another chicken. It doesn't sound so idyllic now does it?

Most horse owners dream about having their horses at home where they can see them out of the window. But things do not always go to plan! A property needs to be managed sustainably otherwise it will very quickly degrade.

But the good news is that the first vision is very achievable if you take the time and due diligence in choosing the right property, in the right place, for the right price. If you know what to look for and what to avoid, you will save yourself (and your family) a lot of potential heartache, not to mention expense.

The most common mistakes that people make when buying a horse property include:

- Failing to thoroughly check out access to riding areas, tracks or trails etc. This is very important if you plan to ride off the property.

- Failing to check out the availability of local horse services i.e. equine vets, farriers or trimmers, hay, feed suppliers etc.

- Failing to find out zoning and other regulations for the area in which the property is situated.

Make sure you check out the availability of local horse services in the area that you are thinking of buying. You never know when you may need a vet or other equine professional.

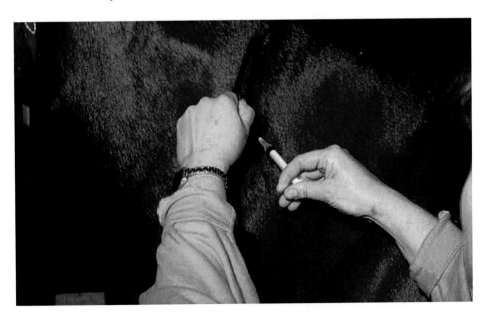

- Failing to thoroughly check out the quality and availability of water supply to the property.

- Failing to check out the local area for potential problems, for example, a commercial chicken farm nearby or a new proposal for a quarry etc.

- Underestimating the effect that living in a rural area will have on the rest of the family, including underestimating the impact of extra travel time to work or school etc.

- Underestimating the time, money and effort required to upkeep a rural property.

- Getting carried away with the horse facilities on a potential property only to find that they are not suitable after purchase.

Some people underestimate how much time, money and effort it will take to upkeep a rural property.

The previous points and many others are covered in this book so that you will be aware of them and will be able to make a much more informed decision. The old saying 'buy in haste, repent at leisure' is very appropriate when buying a horse property, so time spent at this stage is time well spent.

Make sure you think carefully about exactly what sort of property you want/need because changing your mind will not be an option once you have bought it.

Firstly there are some essential questions to ask yourself *and* the rest of the family because there are some very important lifestyle decisions to make. Spend time at this stage thinking about what type of property you want, where you want it to be and what you want to do with it.

Roughly speaking people looking to move to a rural area to keep horses fall into one of three groups:

- Families looking to change to a rural lifestyle. In this case numerous horse facilities may not be too important but proximity to schools and/or the ability to commute to work usually is.

- More serious enthusiasts who are looking to increase their involvement but still work outside the horse industry. This group is probably the largest group and they are usually looking to end up with various horse facilities *and* proximity to schools and/or the ability to commute to work.

You need to think about those requirements necessary for the specific lifestyle you have in mind.

- Professional horse people who know what they need to run a horse business. This group needs specific facilities (or the ability to build them) and may also need staff facilities, access for large vehicles etc. A further complication may be that some members of the family still need good proximity to schools and/or the ability to commute to work.

The needs of other family members are very important when thinking about moving. A very common scenario is for families to move out to acreage and then return to suburbia in the future because certain family members are not happy living a long way out.

Some of the questions to ask yourself and the family might include the following:

- How far can you and your partner realistically afford to live from your work places (if one or both of you will still be carrying on working) and which regions can you actually afford to live in without making too many compromises in other areas of your lives?

- How far away from suburbia or a town or city will the rest of the family be happy to live? Do the areas that you are considering have access to schools, shops, leisure and entertainment facilities?

- Is a larger area of land or a larger house the priority? If you want both then obviously this will cost more and/or you may need to even live further out in the country.

- How many horses or other animals are you planning to keep? More animals mean more land and again either a larger price tag or a more remote situation.

- What is the acceptable distance from good riding areas and proximity to a pony club and/or adult riding club?

Before you start looking at properties for sale, discuss these issues with your partner and the rest of the family. You can now start to formulate your 'wish list'. Near the end of this book there is a general check list that you can take with you when you go to visit properties for sale; add your personal 'wish list' to this. You should find that you add more points as you go through this book - along with any features that you would class as 'absolutely not'.

Compromise will become an important word in your vocabulary because invariably there will be compromises to be made on your ideal property. Just which compromises you are prepared to accept will be crucial in enabling you to find a property that ultimately meets your needs, those of your family and your horse pursuits.

Is a horse property a good investment?

Buying a horse property is probably going to be the largest investment you will ever make so you need to be sure it is a good one. Due to a horse property usually costing more than a suburban property it can take longer to sell if you ever decide to move again (there are usually less buyers available for a more expensive property). However, if you buy a good property in the first place there should be good demand, even when the market is moving slowly. It will at least have a competitive advantage compared to properties that have serious flaws. Equestrian pursuits are currently on the rise in most of the developed and developing world so for now at least, there is great demand for horse properties in many countries.

A horse property is usually a very good investment as long as you buy a good property in the first place, or at least one that has potential.

Renting a horse property is also an option for people who want to move to acreage but cannot afford a high price tag. If you are able to afford (or already own) a property in the suburbs consider renting that out and renting a horse property instead (renting a horse property can be *relatively* cheaper than paying a mortgage on it). This way you still keep your foot on the property ladder, without the higher mortgage payments. If you are planning to run a business on or from the property you need to check if there are any tax incentives verses buying (or vice versa).

Only you can decide if buying a horse property will be a good investment for the future. The more research you do before you buy, the more likely you will buy wisely.

Speak to your accountant about this if you are planning to or already run a business from home. There are many advantages to renting before or instead of buying. It gives you and your family a chance to try an area (or indeed a lifestyle) before becoming too committed. The property that you are renting may even come up for sale during your rental period and if you like it and are ready to buy you are in an ideal position to purchase the property.

Aim to 'buy smart' by buying a property that is going to be relatively easy to run otherwise you will spend all of your precious time on just maintenance rather than doing what you love. In fact some people move *back* to boarding (agisting or keeping at livery) their horses after owning a horse property simply because of the time it takes to maintain a property. So in this example a horse property was not a good investment.

Aim to 'buy smart' by buying a property that is going to be relatively easy to run.

Finding a horse property

Where can you look to find properties for sale? The offices of realtor/real estate (selling) agents are a good place to start. These agents also advertise in newspapers, on the Internet and even in some equestrian magazines. Private sellers (people who manage the sale of their own property without using an agent) also use these forms of advertising. Scour the advertisements and be creative in your approach.

We once found a fabulous property, for private sale, in a tiny classified advertisement tucked away in a rural newspaper. The advertisement only stated that the property was 'suitable for walkers' when in fact it was 70 acres of good grazing land backing onto a large public forest that had access for horse riders! The owners, being unaware of what horse owners see as high priorities, had not known what to point out as one of the property's best features.

The majority of properties that are for sale are already listed with a selling agent, as most people still prefer to use the services of an agent to sell. These agents act as a 'go between' for a buyer and a seller. Agents range enormously in the level of service that they give. If a property is listed with an agent then bear in mind that he/she is working for the seller (because the seller is paying the agent to sell the property for them). It is sometimes possible to find someone who will find a property for you (they may be called a real estate broker or similar).

Some selling agents provide this service but make sure you (and they) are clear about who they are working for (the buyer *or* the seller, otherwise there may be a conflict of interest). This is becoming a more popular concept, and can be invaluable if you are looking for something special (such as a horse property as opposed to a simple suburban house) and especially if you are busy or live far away.

Some selling agents specialise in rural properties and some specialise further by selling only horse properties.

Some agents specialise in rural properties (or even horse properties in particular) and can be a wealth of information. But some agents, particularly those that are based on the urban fringe, do not have a good understanding of the issues involved with acreage properties, most of their experience being with houses in suburbia. These agents may encourage you to look at properties that are far from ideal. This can become frustrating, especially if you have to travel a distance to view properties; however you will build a picture over time of certain areas and their suitability and also certain agents and how to read between the lines of what they tell you.

As already mentioned earlier some properties are listed for private sale by the owner. Private sales can work well as they have advantages for both buyers and sellers. Because there are no agents' fees involved the price of the property may be slightly lower or more negotiable than a property listed with an agent. As a buyer you are able to speak directly with the seller which is important with an acreage property (see the next section **Viewing a horse property**).

You should also put word out among your friends if they live in the area in which you are planning to buy and ask them to tell their friends. They may hear about a property that is about to come up for sale. Finding a property just before it goes on the market can be a big advantage for both parties.

To reduce your chances of making the wrong decision, have a look at as many horse properties as possible, even before you are ready to buy. For example, look out for open days or auctions on properties for sale in the area in which you are interested in (some selling agents do this and some don't). Just looking at properties is a good way of starting to build a picture of what you like or dislike and it is an ideal opportunity to gather ideas on property designs without wasting the agent's time as they have to be there for open days or auctions anyway. If any of your friends own a horse property aim to have a look at that too.

Whenever looking at a property, look with a constructively critical eye. What do you like or dislike? What would you change or do differently? When talking to people who already own a horse property, ask them if they have any tips and if there is anything they wish they had known before they bought their property.

Where should you start to look at properties for sale? There are various options.

It is a good idea in this initial phase to drive around an area that you may be interested in, as this gives you a feel for the area. If possible visit local riding and/or pony clubs and chat to people while you are there. Local people are often an invaluable resource when looking for a horse property. One of them may even know of a potential property that is about to come up for sale. Shop owners and in particular local horse feed or farm supply store owners are also usually good people to talk to.

People who already live in an area can give you a lot of information that a sales agent might not be able to. For example try to find out how easy it is to get local contractors and horse professionals in the area. While you are in the area you can call on local selling agents to give them your details and start to build a picture of what is available and the prices of properties for sale etc.

Prior knowledge about an area helps when an agent contacts you about a property for sale. You will already have an idea about where the property is and you may even have passed by it previously. This approach is obviously less viable if you are buying from far away or overseas. In this case, unless the market is moving quickly, it is usually better to rent a property in the area that you are considering before buying in that area (see the previous section *Is a horse property a good investment?*).

Spend time driving around and getting to know the area that you are considering. This will pay dividends when it comes to making a decision.

The more properties you see at these early stages the better you will become at spotting plus points and potential problems when you start looking in earnest. When you are ready to buy and you do find a property that is for sale you will be able to make a more rapid and informed decision.

By doing your homework first you will be able to refine your search and reject properties at the early stages if they are unsuitable, eventually buying the right property, in the right place, for the right price.

You need to remember that different people value different things; what makes a good horse property depends on an individual's personal preference or viewpoint and indeed what they do with their horses. For example, a person whose chosen sport is dressage may not mind that a property does not have good riding trails nearby (although some dressage riders quite rightly enjoy taking their horses on trails). Whereas an endurance rider will need to train their horses over distance and varied terrain therefore will usually only consider a property with access to good riding trails. In other cases, while some people are happy to compromise on the house to have better horse facilities, others are not.

You need to remember that different people value different things; what makes a good horse property depends on an individual's personal preference or viewpoint and indeed what they do with their horses.

Viewing a horse property

When you start to look at properties for sale consider getting advice if it is available. This may save you a lot of time, money and effort in the long run. This advice could be in the form of a consultant (quite rare), or even in the form of a more experienced friend; someone who has owned or set up a horse property before. Even advice from a friend who is not 'horsey' can sometimes be useful, especially about some of the more practical aspects of a property, as they are not going to be as influenced by 'nice horse facilities' etc. and may be able to see a property for what it actually is.

Aim to get a second opinion on a property. It is hard not to get carried away by the sight of desirable facilities etc. Even advice from a non-horsey friend can be useful, especially about some of the more practical aspects of a property as they are not going to be as influenced by horse facilities etc.

A horse property can become a sponge for money and time so it is important that you choose wisely before you buy.

When you find a property that you are interested in and might wish to pursue it is important that you arrange to speak to the owner rather than relying on the agent alone to answer your important questions. Keep in mind that the agent is trying to sell a property that they may only have previously seen for an hour or so. A horse property is far more complicated than a simple suburban or town house so you need to ask more questions and only the current owner will be able to answer many of these.

Don't be afraid to make arrangements to revisit a property several times before making a final decision even if, or especially if, you are completely convinced that this is your ideal property.

Take your time if you can before making such an important decision.

The exciting subjects

This section covers the subjects that a horse person is most likely to get excited about. Subjects such as whether to buy an already established horse property or whether to buy a blank canvas. There is so much to think about including property location and size, existing facilities etc.

Your budget

The majority of buyers are looking for roughly the same type of property. Between five to twenty acres of flat to undulating land, good water, a nice house, horse facilities and not too far from a town or city. This makes properties that fit this bill very sought after and therefore relatively expensive.

You need to think carefully about your budget and how this is going to affect your hopes and dreams.

Your budget is usually one of the biggest influences when it comes to deciding which property to buy. So you need to work out how much money you will have available after you have factored in any selling costs of your current property and the buying and moving costs of a new one.

It is unlikely that you will find a property that has *everything* on your wish list (unless you have an unlimited budget). However, as long as it has the features that are most important to you, you may decide you can compromise on the others. You can always make improvements later or use the property as a stepping stone to buying another one in the future (as long as you buy wisely).

If your budget is tight then make sure you are not buying a property that has features that you do not really need, for example a professionally constructed arena or riding ring when you only plan to trail ride.

Make sure you do not end up buying a property with lots of features that you would like, but don't really need.

The more horse facilities a property has the more it will cost to buy. Also if you are borrowing to buy the property you will be paying interest on features that you are not using. Facilities tend to degrade over time so you will have wasted money and time spent earning that money, in paying for facilities that you have not used. A surfaced riding area is a good example, in that, if you are using it regularly it is easier to maintain than if you are not. Weeds will grow on a surface that is not in use, which if left to grow, will ruin it. You may also end up with a property that has lots of facilities that are 'human centric' rather than 'horse centric', meaning that many traditional horse facilities do not take the real needs of horses into consideration.

See our book *Horse Ownership Responsible Sustainable Ethical* for more information (available from our websites www.equiculture.com.au and www.horseridersmechanic.com).

An arena will degrade unless it is regularly maintained.

Conversely it is sometimes possible to get a bargain property if the previous owners have over capitalized and need to sell. As long as you are aware of the value of the land if it was undeveloped, plus the cost of the added facilities you can work out if the property is a good buy and make your decision based on that.

When looking at a property you need to ask yourself is it good value for money? Remember you are looking to buy smart. Take into account all the features that will save or cost you money in the future. Compare the price of this property with any others in the area that have sold recently. Selling agents are able to tell you exactly how much properties in the area have sold for in the past (market appraisal), not just the ones that they have sold, because they have access to computer programs that tell them the sold prices of all properties. There are also various websites where you may be able to obtain the information for yourself, but you will probably have to pay, whereas a selling agent will often provide this information for free. Remember however that it is sometimes difficult to value a rural property as each property has unique features unlike a house in the suburbs or city which may be very similar to many others.

If you need a mortgage, what is the amount that you will need to borrow and therefore how much will it cost to service the loan? Keep in mind that some country areas are more difficult to obtain finance for than others. Some lending institutions (banks etc.) are wary about lending money on rural properties. You may need a larger deposit than you would with a suburban property particularly if the property in question is a larger acreage. If it is a bare plot (no house) you may not be able to borrow much at all, if anything, depending on your personal financial circumstances. Shop around the lending institutions, particularly ones that have outlets in rural areas as these will be more helpful about rural properties. Do not be put off if one says no, as lending institutions are very different in their attitudes to rural properties, their terms of lending and the amount they will lend.

You need to calculate the cost of the facilities, how much longer they will last before they will need to be replaced and decide if the price of the property is fair given how much the current owner has spent on it.

The sort of property that you end up with will also depend on other factors including the availability of local trades' people (contractors) and your own skills, abilities and willingness to have a go when it comes to improving a property should this be needed. Do not forget the more rural a property, the more difficult (and sometimes more expensive) it may be to get the trades' people you want, when you want, with limited choices.

Another factor to keep in mind is that even if you are expecting to live on the property indefinitely it is a good idea to buy something that will be reasonably easy to sell if need be. Avoid a property that has features that would commonly be regarded as 'unique'. For example, you and the previous owner may love the fact that the house is built in the style of a medieval castle, but many others may not. You never know when you may have to change your plans and move on.

Property location and size

It is a good idea to arrange your wish list in order of importance and the location of the property should be high on your list (remember the selling agent mantra, Location, Location, Location).

The location and size of a property tend to be related subjects because land becomes more valuable the closer it is situated to a town or city, therefore because most people have a limit to their budget a common decision is whether to go for a larger property further out or a smaller property nearer town.

You need to be sure about how far away you can afford to live from work, shops etc. And remember that the further out you live the harder it can be to get hold of trades people and horse professionals such as equine vets etc.

Remember, if you plan to keep working in the same job once you have moved you need to decide how far away from your place/s of work you can realistically live. It is no good buying your dream property then spending lots of precious time driving between the property and your workplace, not to mention wasting fuel. Also, other family members may not be too enthusiastic about being so far out of town, unless they are also keen horse lovers. Non-horsey teenagers in particular may not appreciate a move to the country and they will need their parents to taxi them pretty much everywhere until they are old enough to drive themselves.

It is no good buying your dream property then spending lots of precious time driving between the property and your workplace, not to mention wasting fuel.

These kinds of pressures can negate the reduction in stress that living in the country is supposed to bring. As mentioned earlier, it is a common occurrence for people to move out to a rural area and then move back to suburbia a couple of years later when it all gets too much.

Think about how much acreage you actually need. Larger is not necessarily better. Good management of a property is a large factor that determines how many animals can be kept in a given area, so in some cases you may not need a larger property but a better management system (see our websites **www.equiculture.com.au** and **www.horseridersmechanic.com** to learn about our other publications which cover how to manage a horse property sustainably). Equally you need to think ahead to the next five to ten years at least. Even if you have just two horses now you need to have a plan for when they retire and you may take on two more horses as replacements.

Keep in mind that the smaller the property the more space a house and any buildings take up relative to the total size of the property. The house, garden, sheds, yards and any stables can easily use up two acres (almost a hectare). Therefore a five acre property (two hectares) will usually have only three acres available for pasture, a three acre property may only have one acre available for pasture and so on. If an arena etc. is added then there will be even less space available for pasture unless it is a grass rather than a surfaced arena.

Land varies enormously in its carrying capacity (some land is highly fertile 'good land', some is highly infertile). Numbers of acres per horse are often quoted as being between 1 acre per horse in some countries/areas to *at least* 2.5 acres per horse in others. In very dry climates even 2.5 acres per horse would not provide enough pasture to feed a horse. So these figures are very arbitrary because, as already mentioned, how land is *managed* is actually more important than how much land you have (within reason). Keep in mind though that the region in which the property is situated may have regulations about animal numbers per hectare/acre (see the section *Zoning and easements*). Whatever the size of the property in relation to the amount of horses there will still be booms and slumps in the amount of pasture through the different times of year so surfaced 'holding areas' (called different things in different countries such as sacrifice yards, dry lots etc.) will usually be required to help monitor the pasture intake and grazing pressure of horses. These holding areas are preferable to stables in terms of horse welfare (see the section *Horse facilities*).

Surfaced 'holding areas' will usually be required.

Remember that the smaller the property the more relative space the house and facilities will take up.

Look out for some of our other publications (see our websites www.equiculture.com.au and www.horseridersmechanic.com) which cover horse property management in detail, in particular 'The Equicentral System' which we have developed and advocate for environmentally friendly sustainable horse property management. The Equicentral System is a rotational grazing system based around a central point that contains the shelter/shade and water. This system has enormous benefits for your budget, land management and horse welfare.

If you buy a property that is too large it may become a burden as that means more of everything to install, look after and maintain. Also there may be tax implications should you decide to sell in the future (this varies from country to country), so check with your accountant.

Another potential problem with having a larger property is the temptation to take on more and more animals because you have the space for them. Eventually you may end up completely tied to the property and holidays etc. become a thing of the past, or the feed (pasture) runs out and you have too many mouths to feed.

Keep in mind that in any area there are boom times for pasture growth but there will also be droughts and other extreme weather events. During a drought it does not make any difference how many acres you have as none of the land will be producing feed. Lots of people get caught out this way and find themselves with too many animals to feed at a time when feed is extremely expensive (during a drought the cost of supplementary feed escalates).

But do be realistic about how many horses you may end up with and remember that each pasture must have one (and preferably many more) periods of rest each year if you want to maximise the grazing potential and not end up with a dust bowl, mud park or weed haven. You may want to allow for some cross grazing as well (grazing different types of animals) as this practice has many pasture and parasitic worm management benefits.

As plots of land decline in size, the *relative* price per acre/hectare increases dramatically so a larger property does not always cost much more. However many acreage properties (lifestyle as opposed to working farm) are five or ten acres therefore this may be all that is available for sale within reasonable distance of a town or city.

Sometimes a horse property can be found in a suburban area. Why would anyone want to keep horses in suburbia? Keeping horses in suburbia can have its advantages and disadvantages. With careful planning and management horses can be kept successfully in this environment. Some of the advantages of suburbia are obvious ones such as proximity to services such as shops etc. and not having to drive as far to work. Non-horsey members of the family are able to live without the disadvantages that rural living offers for people who have no interest in the countryside.

Horsekeeping in built up areas has its own set of pros and cons. But it can be done successfully if good property management is practiced and care is taken to get along with neighbours.

Some disadvantages of keeping horses in suburbia include the expense of suburban land (therefore such properties tend to be very small i.e. less than three acres), manure management issues (you may have to pay to have manure removed from the property on a regular basis) and proximity to neighbours. One of the biggest problems with neighbours being that they may drop dangerous garden waste, such as lawn mower clippings and cuttings from garden plants, in with the horses (thinking that they are doing the horses a favour and getting rid of their vegetation at the same time). This is a very common occurrence in a suburban situation and can lead to the death of horses through poisoning or colic. A double fence can help as well as signage and fostering good relationships with neighbours.

A horse property in a built up area will need to be particularly well planned and managed. Have a look at our **'Equicentral System'** *for ideas about how to do this (see the back of this book for more information).*

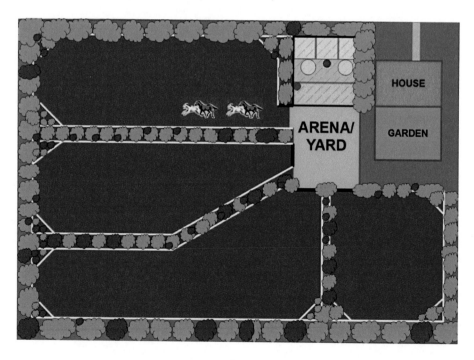

A suburban property will involve a much more intensive system of management than a property in the countryside and it must be kept spotless if a horse owner is not to raise the ire of neighbours. It is usually possible to keep on the right side of neighbours however with gifts of compost (for their gardens) and by maintaining good insect management.

A suburban property will involve a much more intensive system of management than a property in the countryside.

Developed or undeveloped land?

You may have already decided that the property must have existing horse facilities in which case you will not even be looking at undeveloped land, however many people start by planning to buy an established horse property but by the time they have viewed many properties for sale and cannot find what they want they sometimes change their mind. In some urbanised areas and some countries in particular (such as the UK and many other highly populated European countries) it is almost impossible to start with a clean slate so in this case buying an undeveloped plot of land may not really be an option for you.

If you have the choice are you better off buying a property that has few or no horse facilities and constructing them yourself? Or would it be better to buy a property that is already fully operational?

If you have the choice which is the best option? There are advantages and disadvantages to both scenarios. You need to weigh up whether you are prepared to pay the higher cost of buying a property that already has horse facilities but will be immediately usable, against buying a property that has none and you have to build them, or have them built. The second scenario also means that your horse activities may be delayed until the facilities are usable. It can take years to set up a property as you want it to be and meanwhile you (and/or your partner) may run out of steam and/or money.

An established horse property will understandably be more expensive than a property without facilities. Buying an established property can save lots of time in the future, however, unless the facilities are well built and well designed you may be paying an over the top price for the property without realising it. This is a very common occurrence. It is very easy to be bowled over by what seem to be great facilities only to find that they are actually quite shabby and/or badly designed when you start using them after moving in.

If you do find that you do not like the quality and layout of the facilities once you start to use them, changing them will be expensive (plus you will then have paid twice over). It is generally easier to build facilities from scratch than to alter existing ones. This is a very important factor you should consider when buying a property with existing facilities as major repairs are often false economy, even if you have the skills and time to do any alterations yourself (because you should also factor in your own time).

A property that has previously been used for horses may already have land degradation problems such as tracking lines (where horses have walked the fence lines) compacted bare soil and erosion etc. depending on the importance that the previous owner attached to land management. A horse property that has been poorly managed in the past may also have pastures that are 'horse sick', (a result of poor manure and pasture management) whereas a property that has previously only grazed cattle for example should have no horse specific worms in residence. This means that you will be able to start out with good manure and pasture management right from day one and reap the benefits (see the section **Pastures and soil**).

Think very carefully about buying a property that already has serious land degradation problems, even if it is extremely cheap and you have lots of time and energy. On the other hand, renovating a previously poorly managed property can be extremely rewarding.

Sometimes a property is already well fenced but not in a style that you would like, for example, white painted timber fences are nice to look at (if you like that sort of thing, many people don't) but are *very* high maintenance (see the section **Horse facilities** for more about fencing).

Buying a 'bare' plot of land will mean that you can plan and design the property as you like (as long as you get approval).

Make sure you get quotes to change or improve any existing facilities, if that is what you plan to do, before making a decision about buying the property.

If you are looking to buy a 'bare' plot of land it may either have an already designated house site which dictates where you will be able to build the house and other buildings, or you may be free to choose your own house site (subject to municipal council approvals or zoning etc.).

If the plot does have a designated building site check that it suits you, check that the building 'envelope' will be big enough for what you are planning to build and check whether any regulations are in place that will restrict or dictate what you do with the property and what you can and cannot build (see the section **Zoning and easements**). If the plot does not have a designated house site you may need to get professional help to advise you. Some of the factors that help to determine a house site include slope, wind direction, shelter, water supply, soil type (stability), drainage, fire risk, and views, but don't forget access in and out of the property. Remember that a long driveway is expensive to install as are power and phone if the house site is a long way from the road.

Are you prepared to build facilities if necessary? This may delay your horse activities but you should end up with what you want.

Make sure that the land has already had all of the relevant tests or reports completed so that will allow you to go ahead and build. The requirements are varied and numerous and differ from area to area and country to country so speak to the local municipal council and/or your legal representative (solicitor, real estate lawyer, real estate attorney etc.).

See our other publications about horsekeeping systems and planning (available from our websites www.equiculture.com.au and www.horseridersmechanic.com) for more information about how to design the layout of a property for more sustainable land use and healthier horses.

In some countries (particularly the USA) specialized horse communities have been developed whereby the whole development has been planned with horsekeeping in mind. They are developed along similar lines to purpose built golfing and yachting communities and indeed some horse communities also include golfing facilities for example. These developments usually have access to good riding trails and may have facilities such as communal riding arenas and other horse facilities. These horse communities are likely to become more popular over time in countries that have the space to create these large developments.

Again, make sure you do your research before buying because these developments vary greatly in terms of the facilities offered etc. Some of these communities can be very restrictive in what is allowed. Keep in mind that the management structure is limited by the skills and experience of the appointed managers. We have looked at several such communities around the world, and in our opinion although there are some well run equine communities out there, a well managed community is the exception rather than the rule, so make sure that you do your homework before buying.

Another potential scenario is to buy a plot of land that already has a house on it but no horse facilities (but is zoned for horsekeeping).

This type of property will usually be easier to get a mortgage for than a bare plot, but cheaper than a fully developed horse property. This can be a good option provided that the house is positioned well on the land. This option gives you somewhere to live while you get on with developing the horse facilities to your specifications on the rest of the property.

In this case electric fences can be used initially as internal fencing as long as the property has a good solid and permanent perimeter fence. It is actually a good idea to initially use temporary fencing for internal fences as this gives you time to make decisions about where permanent internal fences need to be. Living on a property throughout a cycle of seasons before building permanent internal fences is also a good idea. It means that you will be able to make more informed decisions.

A good solid external fence is a must on a horse property, other than that, electric fencing (permanent and/or temporary) can make up the internal fences.

Horse facilities

If the property already has horse facilities in place you need to be sure that you are not paying for any white elephants which will cost time and money to fix. If there is an arena or other riding surface on the property has it been constructed properly? A riding surface can be either professionally constructed or homemade. Just because a surface is professionally constructed does not mean it will be correctly done and vice versa. There are plenty of good and bad examples of each of these scenarios around. So have a really good look at the surface and ask the current owner of the property questions about its construction (this is just one of those times when you really need to speak to the actual seller rather than just the selling agent). A good riding surface should be able to be used in all weathers and within a few hours of heavy rain. Having a riding surface redone usually costs more than constructing one in the first place so buyer beware!

Are the buildings well built or well converted, safe and user (and horse) friendly? Do any stables look like dungeons rather than being light and airy? Do any outside holding areas (sacrifice yards, dry lots etc.) have an all weather surface on them, which means that they will be able to be used at the time that they are most needed, during very dry or wet weather? Make sure that any buildings or facilities comply with local planning laws before purchase; local authorities are quite within their rights to insist on removal of unapproved alterations.

Check the position of any shelters. They are often in the wrong place. If they are in the wrong place the horses will tend to ignore them and stand where they want to stand anyway.

In this example the shelters have been positioned in such a way that creates unnecessary land degradation (separating horses always causes land degradation but the shelters are adding to the problem). The horses ignore the expensive shelters preferring to stand in sight of each other and where they can see the supplementary feed coming from. The shelters should be where the horses stand.

Fences can be a problem on a property that was developed for animals other than horses. In the case of undesirable or unsafe fences you will need to either re-fence before moving your horses on to the property or use temporary electric fencing to keep them away from the fences until you are able to re-fence.

Fencing generally has a limited life span so make sure you are not paying for fences that have already reached the end of their useful life. You need to budget for this because they will take time and money to remove (plus you may be left with difficult to dispose-of materials) and of course will be expensive to replace. Also consider the layout of internal fences, they may not be in an ideal position, therefore you need to factor in the costs and time required to change them.

If all of the fences are in a poor state or in the wrong position it may cost you many thousands to re-fence the property. Fences should separate wet land from dry land (changes in land type) and any waterways should be fenced off from the grazing areas in pastures (so that vegetation can grow uninterrupted and filter nutrients before they reach the waterway). Electric fencing can help to redress some fencing mistakes or omissions but if these are extensive do you really want to have to bother?

A longer term solution can be to plant trees and bushes in rows on the inside of any undesirable fences, with either an electric fence or simple solid fence (such as posts and plain wire) to keep horses away from the trees and the undesirable fence. This way you end up with a double fence which also provides the numerous benefits of vegetation such as habitat for wildlife (which in turn can help to control pests such as flies and midges or mosquitoes), a highly visible barrier, a space between animals in adjoining pastures, a windbreak, fodder (depending on the type of vegetation) and shade for stock etc. for less money than replacing the undesirable fence with a single width 'horse fence'. Established hedges, for all of the above reasons, are a boon on a horse property so these

should be regarded as a major plus point. See the back of this book for information about where you can buy our other publications on the subject of Sustainable Horsekeeping.

Any fences should be well constructed and suitable for horses (picture left). Everyone has different opinions about what makes a good safe horse fence. Most importantly you do not want to be paying for fences that will need replacing soon after you move in. An old dairy cow shed that has been successfully converted into stables and a tack room (picture right).

A property that was originally developed for animals other than horses can often be successfully recycled into a horse property. For example, well built cattle yards also make good horse yards in many cases. But check out buildings in case the head room is too low for large horses.

Property layout

No two properties are the same and when you go to view properties you will see some *interesting* layouts. Sometimes there is a good reason for the layout of a property that at first sight appears to be unusual. The facilities may have (or should have) been placed to take into account wet areas, microclimates etc., however, some properties are just simply badly designed due to being built on an ad hoc basis without much thought being given to the layout. It is difficult to determine these factors in a short visit and this is another one of those times where you can learn a lot by speaking to the current owner. In order to gain more insight, ask if they built the facilities and why they chose that particular layout.

Make sure the layout suits you. Poor layout can be the cause of future frustration so only buy the property if you think the layout will work.

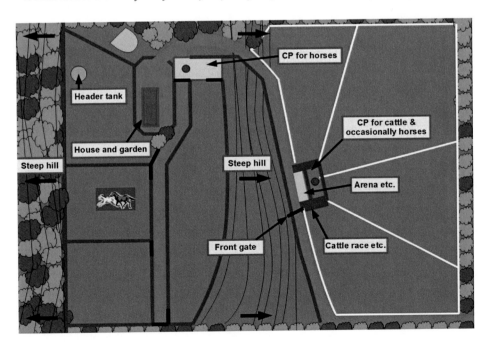

We have other publications about horsekeeping systems and planning (see our websites www.equiculture.com.au and www.horseridersmechanic.com) that will give you some really good ideas about how a horse property should be laid out. In particular about setting up a property so that it is good for horse welfare, good for human convenience and good for the environment all at the same time, a true win-win situation.

Pastures and soil

Be aware that many properties come on the market at the best time of the year, such as when new grass starts to grow in spring, because that is when they look their best. However that same property may be very wet, dry, muddy or dusty a few months later and indeed for most of the rest of the year.

Find out what the land has been used for in the past. If the property has been a working sheep farm there may be old sheep dips on the land which are very dangerous and will need to be removed. The property may have been used for intensive cropping and therefore undesirable chemicals may have been used on the land. If this is the case you need to contact and get advice from the local agriculture department before going any further with a possible purchase.

In fact it is usually a good idea if you can talk to an extension agent or similar (from the local agriculture department) anyway as you will learn various things about the locality that could be very useful.

From a sustainable point of view the best land is land that has not been used for intensive farming or land that has been managed with minimal or no use of chemicals. This kind of land has usually been used for cattle (beef, low intensity) or sheep and as long as it has not been overstocked in the past it should be in reasonably good condition. Keep in mind that some grasses used on cattle properties may not be the best for horses, particularly ex-dairy properties, as the pasture is usually 'improved' and consequently very high in sugar (very dangerous for all but hard working horses). Just because a property is already a horse property does not mean that it will have good pastures either. Many horse properties have 'problem' plants and even more have not had good general pasture management in the past.

The quality of the pastures and soil will affect the amount of feed that can be grown. Good soil is a huge bonus. The soil is often the last consideration of people buying a horse property when in fact it should be very high up the list of important considerations. Good soil will support pasture, grow trees and bushes, require less maintenance than poor soil and will allow you to maintain and further improve your pasture using such strategies as cross grazing. Poor soil can usually be improved however it takes time and expense.

Horse properties often have land degradation problems. Make sure the property is priced accordingly if it has had poor management in the past. The (too) steep pasture is over grazed and the even steeper hillsides are poorly vegetated.

Find out if the soil is clay, loam, sand or gravel. Sandy loam is preferred for pastures and gravely, well drained soils are preferred for buildings, yards and riding surfaces such as arenas. A property with different soil types can be very useful. Wetter areas, if managed properly, produce larger amounts of pasture. These areas will carry on producing grass when the dryer areas of the property have stopped producing. Drier well draining areas are a good place for constructing surfaced holding areas where animals can retreat to when necessary. These drier areas will also be able to be grazed during the wetter times of the year (when the wetter areas of the property will be resting).

You need to know about any surface water problems on the property. When it rains, where does the water flow and where does it settle? If you visit and subsequently buy a property during a dry time of the year it will be more difficult to spot any problems that are due to surface water.

If it rains heavily while you are in the consideration stages of buying a property make sure you get along and have another look at the property during this time. Notice where the water is flowing, if it is flowing straight through the holding areas, stables or across the arena you may have a problem! If the pastures become instant lakes this could also be a problem! Keep in mind though that in some countries such as Australia rainwater does tend to arrive all at once and you do not actually want it to leave just as quickly, it needs time to soak into the land to help plants grow. Many properties require better water management (which can mean earth moving) and earth moving can be expensive so make sure you factor this in. A well set up property in a wet area will have higher and dryer areas that animals can retreat to when necessary.

The Equicentral System that we have developed and advocate works well in this situation. See our websites www.equiculture.com.au and www.horseridersmechanic.com to learn about our other publications which cover how to manage a horse property sustainably.

Ask if the soil has been tested recently. If you know or suspect that the land has been used intensively and/or for some kind of noxious industry you need soil tests before deciding whether to buy or not. Soil tests tell you which nutrients are present and which nutrients are lacking. They will also show chemicals that should not be present (you may want to alert the soil test lab as to why you are having the tests done).

Soil tests will show up problems such as salinity (salinity occurs particularly in the USA and Australia). Visual checks for salinity include looking for scalds or bare patches, or even white crystals shining on the surface (in a bad case). Valleys of cleared land are prone to salinity. Other signs are dead and dying trees, declining pasture i.e. pasture that is very weedy. Ask a local expert or environmental group for advice if you suspect that there is a salinity issue.

Most properties have weeds of one sort or another. Not all weeds are bad (what is a weed to one person is a beneficial herb to another). You must inspect the pastures carefully, don't just stand at the fence looking across the land, a mown pasture always looks good from this angle, even if it is mainly weeds. Walk the land and look to see if the pastures contain mainly grass or mainly weeds. Cut weeds will tend to look 'stemmy' with many spaces between the plants whereas well established perennial (permanent) pasture will still look grassy when mowed. Also be aware that many weeds are only present at certain times of the year so you may not be able to see them at the time of inspection.

Land that has been used for intensive farming may also have chemical residue in the soil. You need to know the history of the land before you make a decision.

Ask what has been done to prevent and control weeds. Look at the land and across at neighbouring properties for evidence of 'declared' or 'noxious' weeds. Again speaking to the local agriculture department or local environmental group will help you to understand what problem plants to look for. Find out how extensive they are in the area, what threat they pose to the land and animals (if any) and how to manage them. Find out who is responsible for eradicating different classes of weeds. Be aware that in some areas you may also be responsible for controlling the weeds on the roadside outside the property.

If weeds are present you need to know how difficult they will be to get rid of. Weeds on horse properties are usually a sign of overgrazing because once grass plants have disappeared the bare soil gives weeds the opportunity to grow. Some weeds are more of a problem than others so you need to be sure about what you might be taking on.

A lot of weeds indicates that the land had been inappropriately managed in the past. The weeds are doing what nature intended them to do, step in when conditions are not right for pasture grasses and repair the soil. So a certain amount of weeds is not necessarily a bad thing although their presence is telling you that the land has not been looked after properly. If the property has many weeds then you need to make sure the property is priced accordingly and that you will be able to manage them and bring the land back to a productive state.

Look out for some of our other publications that cover pasture management in detail. See our websites www.equiculture.com.au and www.horseridersmechanic.com

In addition to lots of weeds, general poor property management would show up as bare compacted areas on the land (particularly in gateways and along fence lines), dirty water in the waterways and erosion.

Poor management also shows up as highly uneven pasture growth with areas of 'roughs' and 'lawns' (caused by poor manure management, pastures in this condition as sometimes referred to as 'horse sick'). Another tell tale sign is unhealthy looking horses, however sometimes a property can be in very bad shape and the horses still look good due to them being fed on supplementary feed.

A property that has previously been used for horses may already have serious land degradation problems such as ring barked trees, bare compacted soil, dirty waterways, weeds etc.

Asking the current owner about how they manage the land will tell you a lot about what land degradation may be present on the property. If the property has been used for a large number of horses (and/or other animals) and good land management practices such as pasture rotation were not carried out then there *will* be land degradation. Even good land cannot cope with continuous pressure from grazing animals without breaks (periods for rest and recuperation). If the previous owner outlines what steps they were taking to manage the property this tells you that they are aware and responsible and are more likely to have done the right things in terms of land management.

Avoid buying someone else's problems unless you have time and money to spare and are able to buy it at a bargain price. If this is to be your first horse property you may want to start with something a little less challenging. At the same time if the property is a good price, turning it into a good sustainable horse property will be an extremely rewarding experience but the price paid should reflect the fact that the previous owners have managed the property poorly.

It is a rewarding experience to improve a property so that it becomes sustainable and supports the grazing of your horses and any other grazing animals you might have.

Natural features

Natural features are a bonus. A property that has a running waterway, mature trees and a natural lake or man made farm dam etc. will have shelter and water already in place and will be a far more desirable property for having them. Trees and bushes are essential on a horse property for shade, wildlife habitat and extreme climate control. Trees and bushes help to keep a property cool when the weather is hot and help to keep a property warm when it is cold. Vegetation takes time to plant and time to grow so the price of a property without any should reflect this.

Fenced off native vegetation such as this is a real plus for a horse property. If it is already in place it will save you having to do it and it will be already well on the way to becoming mature enough to support wildlife such as insectivorous birds which will eat pest insects by the thousands.

The flip side is that if a property does not have already established vegetation you can plant it where you want and will have none to remove if it interferes with building projects.

Trees and bushes that are spread out on a property give a 'park like' look but are more difficult to protect than trees and bushes that are grouped and can be more easily fenced. They also do better when grouped as they help to protect each other from the elements.

Trees that are spread out give a property a 'park like' look but are more difficult to take care of than trees that are grouped. You will need to make sure that the horses do not 'ring bark' the trees as this will kill the trees.

If the property is timbered you will probably not be able to clear it for pasture depending on where the property is and the type of timber. Quite rightly there are more and more restrictions on clearing native timber, and even if and when any timber is cleared you will still have to establish pasture, which can take some time. Pockets of natural vegetation, trees and bushes, on a property that is otherwise cleared are a huge bonus as they provide privacy for the property owners, habitat for wildlife, shelterbelts (i.e. slow down wind) and enhance the appearance of a property etc. It is far better to improve already cleared land (if necessary) and leave pockets of vegetation than to clear them for extra grazing.

A dam or lake is great to have, but it should be fenced off from stock and the water reticulated to where it is needed.

In particular trees and bushes on higher ground produce nutrient rich organic matter (in their leaves) and provide a place for animals to spend time and therefore leave manure (birds in particular). This nutrient rich organic matter then makes its way downhill over time consequently fertilising the land below.

All of these natural features, waterways and vegetation, should be protected by fencing before allowing your horses to have access to pastures. Horses can cause extensive damage in a short space of time to natural features.

Rocky land can be a problem as rocks can make it difficult if working with machinery (such as with a mower/slasher or pasture harrow) on the land. Rocks have a habit of working their way up to the surface continuously so even when an area has been cleared they may still keep popping back up.

Natural ecosystems should be regarded as a huge plus when buying a property. If you are planning to make your property sustainable then the presence of already established natural ecosystems means that you only have to protect them if they are not already protected rather than recreate them. These ecosystems will enhance the lifestyle of everyone and everything living on the property therefore they should be regarded as imperative.

Landscape

Undulations usually mean better views and make a property more interesting aesthetically. A good view can add a lot of value to property however for many horse people the best view of all is to be able to see their horses from the house. This can save time too as you are then able to do quick checks of horses without having to go outside each time. Being able to observe your horses is one of the biggest benefits of owning your own horse property.

A balance of flat land and some undulation usually works best on a horse property. Small hills mean that there will be drier areas on the higher parts of the property in the wetter months. Undulations are also beneficial to horses as they aid in fitness. Steep hills however are not desirable for various reasons. Land that is steep is very difficult to manage. It is harder to manage manure and weeds on steep land and soil erosion is a bigger issue on steep land. Horses should not be forced to stand on sloping ground on a permanent basis as the joints in their legs have no sideways flexion. They are happy to graze on hillsides but prefer to loaf (rest etc.) on flat land (this is one of the reasons that horses, if possible, take themselves to the top of a hill to loaf).

A slope of 2% to 6% is ideal for a horse property, less will tend to be boggy and may be flood prone and more will tend to lead to erosion. If a property is otherwise desirable and has enough flatter land for your needs, steeper areas can be fenced off and vegetated with trees and bushes, or allowed to revert back to natural vegetation, thus turning problem areas into desirable areas. These areas then help to increase fertility on the lower slopes (see the previous section).

Horses are not supposed to stand on sloping ground on a permanent basis. They have no sideways movement in the joints of the legs and can end up with joint problems in the long term.

Look at which way the hill slope faces (the aspect), in the southern hemisphere north facing slopes are sun facing (and the opposite in the northern hemisphere) giving warmth and good vegetative growth. However longer hours of sunlight mean that the grasses will contain higher levels of sugar. This may be a problem if the pasture is 'good' and you have horses that are prone to obesity and its related disorders.

Any excavations (i.e. for a house or shedding and a riding surface) will be more expensive on a slope than flatter land, however, a property that has some steeper land (along with flat) can be planned so that the house is built on the steeper area (there are styles of house that suit steep sites), which will give good views, and the flatter land is developed for horsekeeping, including a riding surface if you are planning to build one.

A balance of flat land and some undulation usually works best on a horse property. Hills mean that there will be drier areas on the higher parts of the property in the wetter months.

Access to riding areas

Many properties are sold as 'ideal for horses' yet they are situated on fast busy roads. If you are not planning to ride off the property at all this may not be a problem but if you plan to ride out finding the right situation is very important. In this case try to find a property that at least has access to quiet country roads (not all country roads are quiet, some have lots of heavy vehicles on them) or better still, direct access to forestry land (with horse riding access) or public riding trails (such as 'rail trails'). Properties with direct access to trails of any kind are very much in demand however, so they can be difficult to find and tend to sell quickly.

Make sure the property has access to good riding off the property if that is what you are planning to do. If that is your priority aim to settle for nothing less!

Source - Carol Layton

If a property backs onto a National Park or similar be aware that you may not be able to ride in there as some forestry lands etc. have restricted (or no) access for horse riders. Find out which government department controls this area and contact them before buying. You can then find out what the access will be to this area (if any) and if there are any plans in the pipeline to change its status. There have been numerous cases of people buying a property because it backed on to a forest and the status of that forest has changed after purchase resulting in them not being able to ride there.

Riding in an arena is fine if that is what you plan to do but not if you wanted to be able to ride out and cannot.

Be aware that if the previous owners were not horse riders they might not know if the nearby forest has access or not, even some horse riders would not know if they mainly ride in an arena. You have to do your own research. Sometimes you may actually get a pleasant surprise.

Sometimes when a property is for sale the seller might explain that there is access to a public forest (for example) but that access is through a neighbour's land, or that the neighbours have always allowed them to ride on their land. Sadly many people end up living within a stone's throw of great riding but cannot access it because this unofficial agreement has broken down. People and properties pass on and the new owners may not extend this agreement to you. It happens quite regularly. It is up to you whether you want to risk it because living near inaccessible riding can be very frustrating.

The district

Try to ascertain what the neighbours are like and what their interests are. If possible try and meet them before deciding on a property. Find out what they do with their land. For example they may have a stallion that is kept in an area backing onto your potential property. If the neighbours do have horses you will probably need to erect a double fence with a bushy screen between them (it is never a good idea to have horses socialising over a fence). They may be motocross bike riding enthusiasts which can lead to problems with noise if they ride frequently. At the same time don't assume that just because the neighbours have horses that you will all get along just fine. Sadly it is often not the case.

The neighbours may have an unusual pastime that might or might not affect your plans.

Is the next door property messy? This might not be a problem in the short term however it may make your potential property difficult to resell in the future, especially if the mess creeps nearer to your property over the years. If the property next door has not yet been built on, try to find out where the house will go. Sometimes people build very close to the fence line on acreage which will mean that your property has reduced privacy (privacy being one of the benefits of living in the countryside).

You need to know all the pluses and minuses of a district. Find out if there are any wind farms, a power station, a mobile phone tower etc. nearby. Even if you do not mind the presence of such things (and let's face it in many cases they have to be *somewhere*) you need to know about them in case they affect the value of the property in question. Also find out about any possibly noxious industries such as intensively managed pig farms, feed lots, slaughter houses and battery chicken/egg farms etc. Unless these properties are practising sustainable management systems there may be an enormous amount of flies in the area and bad odours especially on the days that sheds are cleaned out. Crop and fruit farms can also be a problem if they spray chemicals (unless they are organic they *will* use sprays and even organic farms sometimes use sprays, just different ones).

Spend time researching the wider area that surrounds the property. It is far better to find out that there are things about the area that you do not like or will not work for you and

therefore reject the property at this stage than to buy the property and then be stuck with it.

Most people are aiming for a good compromise between privacy, position, nearness to amenities etc. Each property will have pros and cons that you have to weigh up.

The access

Make sure that the property has suitable all weather access. Any steep dips in the driveway (such as over a waterway) may be impossible for a long wheelbase feed, hay or water truck or a vehicle pulling a trailer, to access plus they are likely to be impassable in wet weather. If the property access is difficult, get quotes (before committing to buying the property) to see how much improvements will cost.

Make sure that the access is suitable and safe. Large vehicles may need to enter and exit the property on a regular basis.

Make sure gateways are wide enough for vehicles to pass through. Can emergency vehicles access the property? Can work vehicles move around the property if necessary? Is there a laneway system in place within the property? If so are the lanes usable in wet weather?

Beware of buying a property where the only entrance/exit has poor visibility when pulling out on to the public road. When pulling out of a property when towing horses or in large vehicles you will need to move much slower than when not, so the entrance must allow for this, especially if the road is busy. Likewise the entrance should allow room for a vehicle and trailer to pull off the road and idle while the driver opens the gate to enter the property.

If the property is situated on a 'dirt' road find out who owns it and who is responsible for its maintenance. Usually this is the local municipal council and it is maintained by them but you need to know if this is not the case and what would be expected of you in this scenario. Sometimes a property shares a driveway with another property or access to the property in question involves access across another property. These situations are often a source of disagreement between neighbours so check out the situation very carefully before you buy.

Make sure larger vehicles can get to and from the property.

Miles of unpaved roads leading to a property are a double edged sword (common in Australia, New Zealand and the US). They will reduce the amount of passing traffic which means that they will be safer to ride on. But they may also mean that at certain times of the year (when it is very wet) it is difficult for you and your family to leave or return to the property.

If the property has narrow lanes leading to it (common in Europe) think about how difficult it may be to get from the main road to the property in a large vehicle (i.e. when towing horses or driving a horse truck). Having deliveries made in large trucks will be problematic or impossible in this situation too.

Unpaved roads leading to a property are a double edged sword.

Climate

The climate can be a very important factor when deciding where to move to. Indeed people move across continents just to live in a better climate. Even though the climate for a particular region is reasonably predictable there can be variations (micro climates) within a region so you need to find out both the macro *and* micro climate of where the property is situated. For example some areas are windier than others and some tend to miss out on rain on a regular basis. To find out such things speak to the locals if possible. Some of the things that are useful or in some cases essential to know about an area include:

- Annual rainfall.
- Amount of frost.
- Length of the growing season.
- Temperature extremes.
- Altitude (higher is generally colder).
- Prevailing wind direction and conditions.

Very wet conditions will mean that the land needs more protection. Surfaced holding areas will be a must in such climates.

Storm, fire and flood risk

Before buying a property it is imperative that you find out the risks of natural environmental disaster in that area. Many areas are at risk of forest or grass fire (a very serious problem in hot countries). Many properties are also at risk of flood or violent storms, hurricanes or cyclones. In fact some localities in various parts of the world are prone to all of these and more (such as earthquakes). The design of a property should account for the probability of their occurrence and the impact that they will make.

If you buy a flood prone property you will need a flood plan and may need extra resources to keep your animals safe.

All properties should have a plan in place for such occurrences if they are at all possible. If you buy the property and the previous property owners have emergency plans, make sure you ask for copies of them, you can then use these to form the basis of your plans.

Some of the questions that you need answers to are:

- What are the likely natural disasters for the area?

- Has there ever been a flood, fire, other natural disaster?

- Where are the emergency services situated? (i.e. how close is the nearest fire department?).

- Is there a community group (to do with disaster preparedness and management) in the area that you should be aware of if you buy the property?

Many areas are at risk of forest or grass fire.

Pest problems

Speak to locals to find out if the area is prone to certain pests such as problematic ticks or larger than normal numbers of flies, midges or mosquitoes. For example properties that are situated near chicken or egg farms can be inundated with a type of fly that is often called a stable fly but actually breeds most prolifically in chicken manure. Most areas have some kind of pest but some areas have a particular problem with a certain pest, especially if an ecosystem is disturbed resulting in certain pests becoming dominant. For example if the habitat for a certain insectivorous bird or insectivorous bat species has been destroyed then there will be more of the type of insect that that bird or bat would normally eat.

Some areas are much worse for biting pests etc.

Sometimes certain animals are regarded as 'pests' even though they are native to that area, for example in Australia and the US some areas have unusually large numbers of native snakes. In parts of Australia native fruit bats can be a problem for horse owners because they carry a very dangerous virus that affects people (via horses) as well as horses. You need to find out what is likely to be a problem in the area that you plan to buy and do your research. The Internet is a good place to start in this case.

Some areas have unusually large numbers of native snakes.

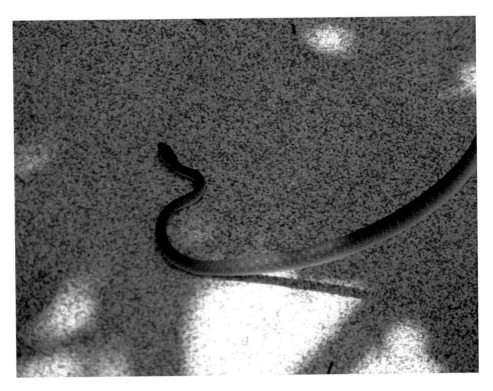

Water supply

Water is an extremely important commodity, in fact you could say that it is *the* most important because without water life is not even possible. A common scenario with water is that there is not enough for weeks on end but then when it does arrive it all arrives at once! On a country property without piped water, water will have to be purchased if it runs out and there is no rain around (common in Australia where rain water is collected in holding tanks). This will be expensive if you are watering stock in addition to domestic usage so it is imperative that the property is self sufficient for water. Firstly, find out how water is provided to the property at the moment. The best scenario is if the property has more than one supply i.e. piped water *and* rainwater storage tanks for example. The more options there are the more the property will be worth.

Properties in suburbia or semi rural areas (and even in fully rural areas in some highly populated countries) usually have piped water. If the property has only piped water and you end up buying it you could plan to install rainwater storage tanks on any buildings to catch rainwater run off that can then be used for watering animals etc. Horse properties usually have a lot of potential for collecting rainwater as they tend to have many buildings with roofs.

Sometimes a property relies totally on rainwater tanks and this water is used for domestic purposes and may be used for the horses and other animals (if there is no other water supply). People who have only ever lived with piped water are often wary about how they will cope with 'tank' water. Unless the property is in a very dry area and as long as there are enough tanks on the property, tank water is not usually a problem. Indeed if you want to live in the countryside you will need to learn to live with tanks in certain places (such as rural Australia). Ironically many country people are wary about piped water! Check the condition and size of any tanks that are on the property because repairing them or buying larger ones will be expensive. Rainwater storage tanks are becoming popular in many countries other than Australia (even when a property has an existing water supply) such as the US and the UK for example because they are a sensible and sustainable way of collecting water that would otherwise run off and be wasted.

Rainwater storage tanks are becoming popular in many countries such as the US and the UK because they are a sensible and sustainable way of collecting water that would otherwise run off. They are already commonly used in Australia.

Bore/well water varies in quality and it should only be used as domestic drinking water if it has been tested and passed as safe to do so. Bores and wells draw water from below ground. If the property does not have a bore/well, find out if neighbouring properties have one, which means that you may be able to install one (you need to check with the local authority first, some localities restrict the installation of new bores/wells because they use ground water which is running out in some areas). You may not need one but it is good to know that you can install one if necessary. Some bore/well water contains trace elements and minerals which may cause harm to humans or animals or land if used for irrigation therefore it is important that you have any such water tested before using.

Farm dams or lakes can be used for watering stock and if water is scarce they can also be used for some domestic purposes such as flushing toilets. Dams or lakes should ideally be fenced off and the water pumped (reticulated) to holding tanks from where the water can be distributed to where it is needed. By fencing off a farm dam or lake and reticulating the water into storage tanks, (especially in times of plenty), you will improve the quality and longevity of the water. If there is a water pump in place ask if that will be staying with the property when the property is sold. Check any farm dams for signs of leakage. Dams that leak can be expensive to fix.

If the property borders a running waterway the property may or may not have a license to pump water from it. It is not automatic that a property has rights to draw water so do your research. There may be a pump already in operation (but again this does not mean it is legal). Ask if the pump is included with the property. Find out which body has control of the waterways in the area in which the property is situated and check out the situation thoroughly.

If well managed, farm dams and lakes are a haven for wildlife, a source of clean water and a real asset to a property. Water is a very precious commodity indeed. It is a privilege to have a good water supply and it must be cared for if it is not to end up spoiled.

Just because a waterway runs through or past a property does not mean that it will run all year. In fact if it is described as 'seasonal' or similar this means that it will dry up in the drier part of the year (which may be the largest part of the year). It also means that it may be a raging torrent when it rains. It is not uncommon for a seasonal waterway to become deep fast moving water for short periods of each year (common in Australia).

This is another reason to hold off putting up permanent internal fencing if you do buy the property; you need to see where any potential flooding may occur before risking fencing, or more importantly risking horses, being washed away!

Check out any irrigation if the property is set up for it, (ask to see it working). The water used for irrigation is usually supplied by a bore/well or a river (or in some localities by a farm dam or lake).

If a property does not appear to have enough water then you need to calculate the costs involved with obtaining and storing more water i.e. buying more rainwater storage tanks or sinking a bore/well. You can than decide if the property is still going to be suitable given the extra expense.

You may need to buy more rainwater storage tanks or sink a bore/well so make sure you factor this in.

Utilities and services

If you are looking at buying a plot of undeveloped land check the availability of power (unless you are planning to use solar in which case you will have to cost in setting up a solar and/or generator system). Just because power is on the property next door does not necessarily mean that it can simply be extended to your potential property. Sometimes an extra junction box needs to be added (which can be expensive). Check with the power company. A new subdivision (where a developer has divided a large parcel of land into many smaller ones) may have power to the front gate. You also need to find out about a phone connection if it is not already connected (unless you are planning to manage without a landline). If so you will need to have good enough reception for mobile (cell) phone and Internet.

If there are no properties with amenities nearby then it may be very expensive to get them all the way to the property. You will need to obtain quotes and base your decision on that.

Check out what is covered by the local municipal council taxes (rates) for the property, for example, sometimes on country properties you have to transport your own waste (rubbish/garbage) away from the property. Find out if there are recycling facilities available.

If the property has a septic tank system for sewerage, find out where it is placed (if this is not obvious). Sometimes the entrance to the septic tank is inadvertently covered over when a garden is landscaped. This is a problem when the septic needs to be cleaned if a new owner does not know where it is.

Keep in mind that horses should be kept away from septic tanks (they have been known to fall in them if the 'roof' of the tanks has collapsed) and they should not be allowed to graze over the drain lines of a septic due to the risks of bacterial contamination.

You may be expected to replace an old septic system with a newer, more eco friendly (and usually quite expensive) system if you apply to make changes to the buildings. You need to factor this in to your budget.

If you are planning on renovating the existing house and making it bigger you may, due to regulations, have to install a new larger septic system or even something else entirely to deal with sewage. Septic systems are being phased out in many areas as they have been superseded by more ecologically friendly systems. This means that when an application is put in to make changes to a dwelling the relevant authority may insist that a completely new system is installed. You need to know these things before you buy and factor them into your costing/budget etc. prior to purchase. Get advice from a local plumber who deals with septic systems about the condition of the current system and the possibility and cost of expanding it or replacing it if necessary.

You need to find out the yearly taxes (rates) for the property in question. These cover such amenities as road maintenance, waste disposal, public area maintenance (such as parks) etc. Rural properties are rated differently depending on such factors as the amount of land and proximity to a town or city. The selling agent or vendor should be able to assist you with these details but check with the local municipal council if you are unsure.

Another thing to check includes mail delivery or whether you would have to open a box for mail (at a post office or elsewhere).

Access to horse specific services

The further out into the countryside the property is situated the harder it may be to get horse specific services such as equine vets, farriers or trimmers, horse dentists etc. If you can get them they may need to either charge much more and/or insist on only coming out to your property for servicing larger numbers of horses.

The exception to this rule is that areas that have large numbers of (usually thoroughbred) studs and training stables are often quite rural (particularly studs). In these areas there will be lots of equine specific services but not all of them will be interested in servicing smaller horse properties. For example it can be difficult to get a farrier or trimmer in such an area as they may be contracted to these large organisations. Equine vets in these areas are usually happy to work with all types of equines but during the breeding season they are often very busy on the studs.

The further out the property is the more difficult it can be to get equine professionals to attend to your horses.

Zoning and easements

Contact the local municipal council and find out the zoning in which the potential property is situated. Zoning controls what is built where so that an area develops in a regular way (or stays undeveloped as the case may be). Zoning establishes certain areas for particular uses such as industrial, rural, residential etc. and also protects environmental areas including water catchments (so that we have clean and safe drinking water into the future). Zoning will also usually dictate factors such as building type and how far a building can be placed from a boundary fence, road or waterway.

You will usually need to get approval before building anything (even an arena or riding ring in some areas) and zoning is one of the regulations that a local municipal council uses to grant or withhold approval. If you build something (such as a house) or construct something (such as an arena or riding ring) without approval, you may be made to take the building down or return the land to its original state at your expense.

Another consideration is that the zoning may prevent you from running an equine business or some other form of business on the property.

Zoning and what it entails, varies greatly from area to area. Find out if the zoning will restrict the amount of horses (or other animals) that you can keep. If possible, find out if the zoning has been changed in the past as this will give you information about the history of the property which could be useful. Find out if there are any plans to change the zoning in the future and how this might affect the property.

Occasionally in more urbanised areas, there are rules in place that stipulate that if a property changes hands, the new owners will have to abide by new regulations. This can occur as a practice by some municipal councils to phase out the keeping of certain animals in some areas. Do not just rely on the views of the selling agent and/or vendor. They may not necessarily be abreast of all the local zoning restrictions and any changes such as those mentioned above.

Check that the zoning for the area (especially in more built up areas) will allow horsekeeping and how many horses are allowed to be kept. In built up areas check that you will still be able to keep horses on the property if you buy it because there may be rules in place that mean the allowed number of animals changes when the property changes hands.

Find out from the municipal council if there are any other restrictions that will affect what you do with the property, for example the area or the buildings may be 'heritage listed' or contain listed buildings, (the terminology varies from country to country) thereby restricting renovation and development. Check out the local terminology. You can initially do a simple Internet search to find out the basics if you think this is going to be an issue. This will give you an idea of what to expect and you will then have a better understanding of any specific clauses etc. that your legal advisor finds if and when they survey the property.

Find out if the property has a 'right of way' running across it (common in Europe). This means that people will be able to walk across your land (and ride if the right of way is a bridle path) on designated paths or tracks. Rights of way and other easements allow people access to land that is not owned by them.

Ask to see a copy of the land title to find out if there are any covenants or easements on the title deeds. The selling agent, or the owner if selling privately, will have a copy of these. If you go ahead and buy the property your legal advisor should also check all of these things for you, but if you find something undesirable at an earlier stage it will save time and expense.

Easements can be for numerous purposes including utilities and services such as power and phone. So for example power lines that run to other properties may cross the property in question and the power company needs access from time to time for maintenance. Easements can also be for many other purposes such as the conservation of certain protected plants, right to light, right to views etc. Go to this link for a good introduction to the subject of easements www.wikipedia.org/wiki/Easement

You also need to find out if there are regulations in force about manure management or if permits are required to keep horses (or other animals). In some countries proof of certain vaccinations are required to move into, and out of, an area.

Find out if there are regulations in force about what you will have to do with manure. Increasingly manure is being seen as a noxious substance and the disposal of it is coming under scrutiny, particularly in urban or semi rural areas.

Even if the local municipal council does not deal with some of these issues directly they should be able to tell you who does. If you are planning on building anything on a potential property you should speak to the planning department *before* you buy the property.

Future proposals for the area

Find out if there are any development proposals in the pipeline at the moment such as road widening, urban expansion, wind farms or a quarry etc. Future developments may be a plus or a minus depending on your viewpoint (for example they may lead to employment for you and your family) and either way you need to know before you buy. Find out if there are any easements planned for the property such as new gas and power lines.

Make sure nothing is about to happen in your chosen area that would ruin your plans for equine utopia.

Find out about the likelihood of mining or drilling for gas etc. in the area and get legal advice if you are not sure.

Find out if the potential property or its neighbouring properties can be, or are likely to be, subdivided later on. Again you may or may not approve of the answer but you need to know at this stage.

A *local* legal representative is more likely to be aware of proposed changes in the area so if you do not already have one it may be a good idea to contact a local one if you decide to go ahead with the purchase.

Find out if the potential property or its neighbouring properties can be, or are likely to be, subdivided later on.

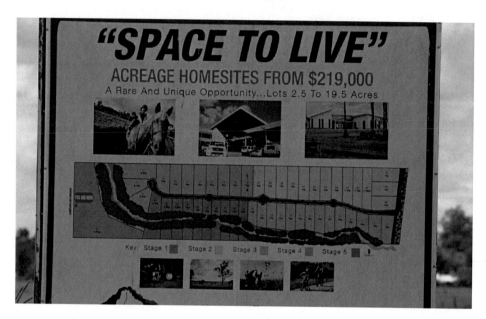

Your check list

You need to make up a list that you can take with you when you visit properties for sale. Below are the main points which will require answers. Add your personal wish list to these points so that you do not forget what are your most important property features:

- Is this property within your budget, taking into account money that will have to be spent on any alterations or improvements?

- Is the house what you want or need, if not will it need many alterations and what will they cost?

- Is the property good value for money?

- Will you able to get a mortgage for this property if you need one?

- If the plot is undeveloped but with an already designated 'building envelope' is the house site where you would like it?

- Will you be able to get or afford power and phone to the house?

- Is the property located in the area you would like?

- Is the property large enough for your needs?

- Is the property going to be suitable for the rest of the family?

- How far away are: schools, shops, workplaces, entertainment, riding trails, riding clubs, extended family and friends, a farrier or trimmer, an equine vet?

- Does the property have good natural features?

- Does the property have a good water supply?

- Is the property steep or flat?

- Are there any out of the ordinary problems with pests?

- What are the risks of fire and flood or other natural disasters?

- Does the property have good soil and pastures?

- Does the property have many land degradation problems?

- Do you like the property layout?

- Does the property have the facilities you need or more than you need?

- Are any facilities well constructed?

- Are the fences well constructed or do they need replacing?

- Does the property have suitable all weather access?

- Does the area have adequate rainfall? What is the climate in the area?

Are the fences well constructed or do they need replacing?

- Does the property have access to good riding areas or trails etc.?

- Does there appear to be any potential problems with the neighbours?

- Are there any zoning restrictions, easements etc. that will dictate or restrict what you build on the property or do with the property?

- Are there going to be other restrictions that would affect your plans?

- Are there any future proposals for the area?

By sticking to your check list you should be able to make the right decision.

The less exciting but still very important subjects

The legals

The legal side of buying a property may not be the most exciting part but it is essential to make sure you are covered and that you are not setting yourself up for future problems.

This publication is intended as a guide only. Between countries and indeed within countries legal requirements vary. At all times consult with local experts on all aspects of the assessment and purchasing of your property.

Plan to have any inspections that are recommended in the property's location (such as termites, damp, building reports etc.). Make sure any building inspections also cover outbuildings such as any stables etc.

If you are happy with the initial checks and decide to go ahead and buy the property you will need to negotiate a price and closing date that is right for you and the seller (see the section *Settlement period*) and you will need to appoint a legal representative (solicitor, real estate lawyer, real estate attorney) if you have not already done so. This is an area that you should not scrimp on; indeed in some parts of the world a lending institution makes their appointment a requirement.

Aim to have your legal representative review and approve the offer you make (via the selling agent or directly to the vender in the case of a private sale) on a property. You can make the initial offer subject to this before you sign a binder. They can then make sure that your rights are protected and your duties clearly defined. Their mission is to negotiate to make a transaction *come together* in a peaceful manner that is fair and amenable to both sides.

A legal representative's role can be as broad as you want. They are usually responsible for services including carrying out thorough checkups with the relevant planning departments and checking that any existing buildings have permits if required. They will also check for any outstanding taxes/rates, liens or builders orders etc. on the property. They will advise which surveys you should have carried out (for example a boundary survey, drainage survey etc.) and will usually arrange these for you. They also review the contract itself and will negotiate repairs based on the building inspection report, and collaborate with the title company etc. Finally they will also be with you at settlement (or be there on your behalf) along with your selling agent and lending institution if applicable. All of these people are working for you to make sure you are protected.

Making sure that any buildings have the correct approvals will save potential heartache later on.

Settlement period

Try to arrange the settlement period to suit you and include any conditions in the contract that you think may be necessary. The settlement period on a rural property is often longer than on a suburban house (although if both parties agree it can be short) because moving can be more complicated (because there are stock and farm machinery to relocate etc.). You may want to stipulate certain conditions such as the septic system to be emptied, any old car bodies, manure heaps etc. to be cleared before settlement. Make sure you negotiate what the property can be used for before you move in because it is common for a property to be overgrazed in the interim period; conversely you may want to arrange that the pastures are mowed just before you move in. You may want to arrange the separate purchase of any extras such as farm implements: tractor, mower/slasher, hay feeders etc. that belong to the current owners.

You may want to stipulate that the pastures are rested and/or are mowed before you move in etc. These kinds of stipulations are important especially if the settlement period is a long one.

Insurance

Find out from your legal representative at what stage you will need to insure the property because during the period between signing an initial contract and final settlement you may be classed as the owner in the event that anything happens to it (even though you have not yet paid in full for the property). Keep in mind that insuring a horse property is much more expensive than a suburban house as there is a lot more to insure. In fact make sure (before you are committed to buying) that the property is insurable because insurance companies do not like certain properties (the ones they regard as high risk, i.e. flood prone or fire prone, especially if they are a long way from fire services). Also an insurance company may only insure the property after certain modifications have been installed.

Nearly there now, just the formalities to sort out and then you, your family and your horses can move in.

Before you move on to the property with your animals you should ensure you have at least third party insurance cover for accidents caused by your animals straying on to the road or other people's properties. Rural property insurers may offer this in with an insurance package i.e. home plus contents plus facilities plus fences and third party for any damage your animals may cause. Make sure you read the small print.

Ensure you have at least third party insurance cover for accidents caused by your animals straying on to the road or other people's properties.

Moving in

Now all you have to do is move in. It may be a good idea to arrange for your horse/s to stay where they currently live for at least a few days longer after you and the family move in. This way you can concentrate on moving in without having to supervise the horses in their new home at the same time. If you do own several horses it may be worth having them moved 'en masse' by a reputable transport company. They will then arrive all at the same time which can be less problematic than separating a herd.

Aim to give the horses several daylight hours the first time they are turned out after arriving so that they have plenty of time to familiarise themselves with their surroundings before dark.

Try to arrange that the horses arrive no later than midday so that they have plenty of daylight hours to get used to their new surroundings. Either way it is a good idea to keep them confined to holding areas or even stables at least for the first night in order to minimise potential accidents. If you only own one horse then be aware that removing him or her from other horses (at their previous home) to a property on their own will create stress for that horse. Horses are herd animals and need other horses for company. In this case you may be better waiting until you have found a companion horse before moving your horse on to your new property.

It is tempting now to sit down with a glass of wine or a beer and savour your new property; however the reality is that now the real work starts! Good luck and have fun.

Further reading - A list of our books

Buying a Horse Property

Buying a horse property is probably the most expensive and important purchase you will ever make. Therefore, it is very important that you get it right. There are many factors to consider and there may be compromises that have to be made. This guide to buying a horse property will help you to make many of those very important decisions.

Decisions include factors such as whether to buy developed or undeveloped land? Whether to buy a smaller property nearer the city or a larger property in a rural area? Other factors that you need to think about include the size and layout of the property, the pastures and soil, access to riding areas, the water supply, and any possible future proposals for the area. These subjects and many more are covered in this book.

A useful checklist is also provided so that you can ask the right questions before making this very important decision.

If you are buying a horse property, you cannot afford to miss out on the invaluable information in this book!

The Equicentral System Series Book 1: Horse Ownership Responsible Sustainable Ethical

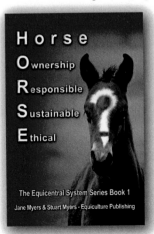

With horse ownership comes great responsibility; we have a responsibility to manage our horses to the best of our ability and to do this sustainably and ethically.

Horse keeping has changed dramatically in the last 30 to 40 years and there are many new challenges facing contemporary horse owners. The modern domestic horse is now much more likely to be kept for leisure purposes than for work and this can have huge implications on the health and well-being of our horses and create heavy demands on our time and resources.

We need to rethink how we keep horses today rather than carry on doing things traditionally simply because that is 'how it has always been done'. We need to look at how we can develop practices that ensure that their needs are met, without compromising their welfare, the environment and our own lifestyle.

This book brings together much of the current research and thinking on responsible, sustainable, ethical horsekeeping so that you can make informed choices when it comes to your own horse management practices. It starts by looking at the way we traditionally keep horses and how this has come about. It then discusses some contemporary issues and offers some solutions in particular a system of horsekeeping that we have developed and call **The Equicentral System.**

For many years now we have been teaching this management system to horse owners in various climates around the world, to great effect. This system has many advantages for the 'lifestyle' of your horse/s, your own lifestyle and for the wider environment - all at the same time, a true win-win situation all round.

The Equicentral System Series Book 2: Healthy Land, Healthy Pasture, Healthy Horses

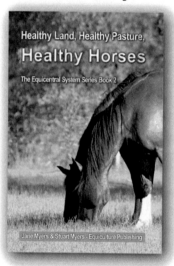

If you watch horses grazing pasture, you would think that they were made for each other. You would in fact be correct; millions of years of evolution have created a symbiotic relationship between equines (and other grazing animals) and grasslands. Our aim as horse owners and as custodians of the land should be to replicate that relationship on our land as closely as possible.

In an ideal world, most horse owners would like to have healthy nutritious pastures on which to graze their horses all year round. Unfortunately, the reality for many horse owners is far from ideal. However, armed with a little knowledge it is usually possible to make a few simple changes in your management system to create an environment which produces healthy, horse friendly pasture, which in turn leads to healthy 'happy' horses.

Correct management of manure, water and vegetation on a horse property is also essential to the well-being of your family, your animals, your property and the wider environment.

This book will help to convince you that good land management is worthwhile on many levels and yields many rewards. You will learn how to manage your land in a way that will save you time and money, keep your horses healthy and content *and* be good for the environment all at the same time. It is one of those rare win-win situations.

The Equicentral System Series Book 3: Horse Property Planning and Development

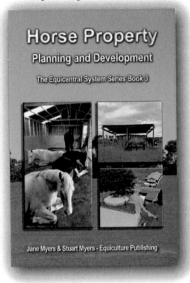

It does not matter if you are buying an established horse property, starting with a blank canvas or modifying a property you already own; a little forward planning can ensure that your dream becomes your property. Design plays a very important role in all our lives. Good design leads to better living and working spaces and it is therefore very important that we look at our property as a whole with a view to creating a design that will work for our chosen lifestyle, our chosen horse pursuit, keep our horses healthy and happy, enhance the environment and to be pleasing to the eye, all at the same time.

Building horse facilities is an expensive operation. Therefore, planning what you are going to have built, or build yourself is an important first step. Time spent in the planning stage will help to save time and money later on.

The correct positioning of fences, laneways, buildings, yards and other horse facilities is essential for the successful operation and management of a horse property and can have great benefits for the environment. If it is well planned, the property will be a safer, more productive, more enjoyable place to work and spend time with horses. At the same time, it will be labour saving and cost effective due to improved efficiency, as well as more aesthetically pleasing, therefore it will be a more valuable piece of real estate. If the property is also a commercial enterprise, then a well-planned property will be a boon to your business. This book will help you make decisions about what you need, and where you need it; it could save you thousands.

Horse Properties - A Management Guide

This book is an overview of how you can successfully manage a horse property - sustainably and efficiently. It also complements our one day workshop - *Healthy Land, Healthy Pasture, Healthy Horses*.

This book offers many practical solutions for common problems that occur when managing a horse property. It also includes the management system that we have designed, called - **The Equicentral System**.

This book is a great introduction to the subject of land management for horsekeepers. It is packed with pictures and explanations that help you to learn, and will make you want to learn even more.

Some of the subjects included in this book are:
The grazing behaviour of horses.
The paddock behaviour of horses.
The dunging behaviour of horses.
Integrating horses into a herd.
Land degradation problems.
The many benefits of pasture plants.
Horses and biodiversity.
Grasses for horses.
Simple solutions for bare soil.
Grazing and pasture management.
Grazing systems.
Condition scoring.
Manure management... and much more!

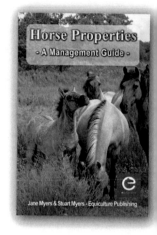

A Horse is a Horse - of Course

Understanding horse behaviour is a very important part of caring for horses. It is very easy to convince yourself that your horse is content to do all of the things that you enjoy, but a better approach is to understand that your horse sees the world quite differently to you, after all, you are a primate (hunter/gatherer) and your horse is a very large hairy herbivore! So it's not surprising that you both have a very different view of the world.

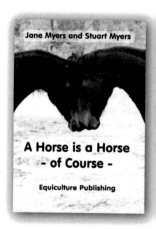

A good approach is to take everything 'back to basics' and think about what a horse has evolved to be. This book describes horse behaviour in both the wild 'natural' environment and in the domestic environment. It then looks at how you can reduce stress in the domestic horse by understanding and acknowledging their real needs, resulting in a more 'well-adjusted', content and thriving animal.

Do your horse a favour and read this book!

Horse Rider's Mechanic Workbook 1: Your Position

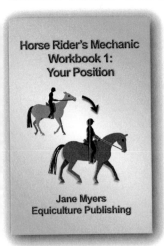

Many common horse riding problems, including pain and discomfort when riding, can be attributed to poor rider position. Often riders are not even aware of what is happening to various parts of their body when they are riding. Improving your position is the key to improving your riding. It is of key importance because without addressing the fundamental issues, you cannot obtain an 'independent seat'.

This book looks at each part of your body in great detail, starting with your feet and working upwards through your ankles, knees and hips. It then looks at your torso, arms, hands and head. Each chapter details what each of these parts of your body should be doing and what you can do to fix any problems you have with them. It is a step by step guide which allows you to fix your own position problems.

After reading this book, you will have a greater understanding of what is happening to the various parts of your body when you ride and why. You will then be able to continue to improve your position, your seat and your riding in general. This book also provides instructors, riding coaches and trainers with lots of valuable rider position tips for teaching clients. You cannot afford to miss out on this great opportunity to learn!

Horse Rider's Mechanic Workbook 2: Your Balance

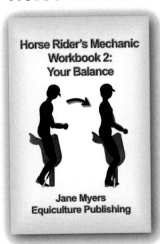

Without good balance, you cannot ride to the best of your ability. After improving your position (the subject of the first book in this series), improving your balance will lead to you becoming a more secure and therefore confident rider. Improving your balance is the key to *further* improving your riding. Most riders need help with this area of their riding life, yet it is not a commonly taught subject.

This book contains several lessons for each of the three paces, walk, trot and canter. It builds on *Horse Rider's Mechanic Workbook 1: Your Position*, teaching you how to implement your now improved position and become a safer and more secure rider. The lessons allow you to improve at your own pace, in your own time. They will compliment any instruction you are currently receiving because they concentrate on issues that are generally not covered by most instructors.

This book also provides instructors, riding coaches and trainers with lots of valuable tips for teaching clients how to improve their balance. You cannot afford to miss out on this great opportunity to learn!

You can read the beginning of each of these books (for free) on the on the Equiculture website www.equiculture.com.au

We also have a website just for Horse Riders Mechanic www.horseridersmechanic.com

All of our books are available in various formats including paperback, as a PDF download and as a Kindle ebook. You can find out more on our websites where we offer fantastic package deals for our books!

Make sure you sign up for our mailing list while you are on our websites so that you find out when they are published. You will also be able to find out about our workshops and clinics while on the websites.

Recommended websites and books

Our websites www.equiculture.com.au and www.horseridersmechanic.com have links to our various Facebook pages and groups. They also contain extensive information about horsekeeping, horse care and welfare, riding and training, including links to other informative websites and books.

Bibliography of scientific papers

Please go to our website www.equiculture.com.au for a list of scientific publications that were used for this book and our other books.

Final thoughts

Thank you for reading this book. We sincerely hope that you have enjoyed it. Please consider leaving a review of this book at the place you bought it from, or contacting us with feedback, stuart@equiculture.com.au, so that others may benefit from your reading experience.

Made in the USA
Middletown, DE
26 May 2017